LAX

DHL Worldwide Courier Services are daily visitors to LAX where they maintain their own depot for their parcel distribution business. Re-engined DC8-73F N803DH is one of seven used by the company on long haul services and complements a large fleet of B-727s.

LAX

LOS ANGELES INTERNATIONAL AIRPORT

FREDDY BULLOCK

Airlife
England

China Airlines flight 006 makes an impressive sight at the end of its long non-stop journey across the Pacific from Taipei. The Boeing 747-409, registered B-164, is painted in the new corporate livery of the airline.

Opposite Above:
After a non-stop flight from Zürich, Swissair's MD-11 HB-IWI is a few moments away from landing on runway 24R.

Opposite Below:
Based in São Paulo, the Brazilian airline VASP fly regular daily services to LAX using their modern fleet of MD-11s. This aircraft, PP-SPE, is on finals for landing on runway 24R after a flight from Rio de Janeiro.

swissair

VASP
PP-SPE
MD-11

Asiana
아시아나항공
ISO 9002

NORTHWEST
1153
NORTHWEST
CARGO

Opposite Above:
Korea-based, Asiana's Boeing 747-48E HL7416 commences its take-off on runway 24L at the start of its return flight to the South Korean capital Seoul.

Opposite Below:
Northwest's DC-10-40 N153US and a Boeing 747 freighter, N630US, are parked side by side awaiting their next call to duty.

Above:
Northwest Cargo's Boeing 747-200F N630US sits in the afternoon sun awaiting its next assignment.

Below:
A Delta L1011 TriStar is pushed back from the gate at Terminal 6 ready for another flight.

Opposite Above:
In order to increase capacity, LAX have constructed several independent satellite terminals situated away from the main terminal building, where passengers disembark and are transferred by bus to the US Customs area. Korean Air Boeing 747-4B5 HL7479 is shown parked at one of these buildings which can accommodate two aircraft, one at either side.

Opposite Below:
Federal Express, now retitled FedEx and based in Memphis, Tennessee, are America's most successful parcel carriers, operating a large fleet of aircraft. Every night they fly back to the hub in Memphis where all packages are unloaded, sorted and re-assembled onto their respective aircraft and flown back in this case to LAX for next-day delivery. DC-10-30F N307FE is parked during the day awaiting its next flight.

HL7479
KOREAN AIR

Fed
FedEx
Federal Express
FedEx

DC-8-73CF N791FT of Emery Worldwide sits in the Californian sun waiting for its next load of cargo to be put onboard.

Opposite:
Chile's major airline Lan Chile operate a DC-8-71F in cargo configuration. After loading is completed this aircraft will return to the Chilean capital Santiago.

LanChile
LanChile Cargo

LanChile Cargo

Western Pacific, based in Colorado Springs, operate their fleet of Boeing 737-300s in an enterprising way by selling advertising space on the exteriors of the aircraft. The example illustrated here features Colorado Tech and looks very colourful on N952WP.

One of Russia's emerging airlines is Transaero. In order to fly long-haul international services they leased three American Airlines' DC-10-30s. In co-operation with the latter they fly twice-weekly from the Russian capital Moscow to LAX. The aircraft shown is being towed to the gate for passengers to disembark.

American
American
Airlines
LuxuryLiner
D
←D10

American
LuxuryLiner
AA

Above:
Resplendent in Air New Zealand's new colour scheme, Boeing 747-419 ZK-NBT lands on runway 24R with NZ18, a non-stop service from Auckland.

Opposite:
American Airlines are one of the major users of LAX with flights to most cities within the USA as well as international flights. With the new Control Tower in the background, DC-10-10 N132AA taxies towards runway 24L for take-off on its flight to Honolulu.

In celebration of 25 years of flying, SkyWest Airlines, a 'Delta Connector' operator, repainted Embraer Brasilia N393SW in a special colour scheme.

United Express operate commuter flights to and from LAX to places like Bakersfield, Palmdale, Palm Springs and other points within southern California. These flights connect with inter-American and international destinations.

UNITED EXPRESS
N201YW

N324AE
American Eagle

Opposite Above:
The United Express Embraer Brasilia N201YW still carries the older United colour scheme as it taxies for take-off with another short commuter flight.

Opposite Below:
American Eagle, like SkyWest and United Express, operate the shorter commuter routes within southern California for its parent company American. Saab 340B N324AE having landed on runway 24R proceeds to the terminal.

Below:
Alaska Airlines, based in Seattle, operate many flights to LAX using a fleet of MD-80s and Boeing 737s. A 400 series Boeing N756AS waits at the gate for passengers to board before its next trip.

Above:
Based in Dallas, Texas, Southwest Airlines are the most successful of America's low-cost flight operators with a large fleet of over 200 Boeing 737s. Several of their aircraft are painted in theme colours, such as N383SW seen here in the state colours of Arizona.

Opposite Above:
United Airlines operate some of their Boeing 737s under the title 'United Shuttle', a low-cost, no frills approach to flying to compete with some of their rivals.

Opposite Below:
DC-8-71F CC-CAX of the Chilean cargo operator Fast Air is on finals to land on runway 25L after a flight from Santiago.

Shuttle
BY UNITED
9377

CARGO

JAL
80

JAL
SUPER
LOGISTICS
JAL

Opposite Above:
Besides operating many passenger flights from Japan to Los Angeles, Japan Air are also regular operators of Boeing 747 freighters. This picture of JA 8180 gives some impression of the enormous size of these aircraft.

Opposite Below:
Japan Air Cargo now operate their fleet of Boeing 747-200 freighters under the title of 'Super Logistics' which is well illustrated here. Having loaded with cargo for its flight to Tokyo, JA 8180 has been pushed back from its ramp area and awaits instructions from the new Control Tower seen in the background.

Above:
Looking resplendent in lovely afternoon lighting, Holland's state airline KLM with their Boeing 747-406 PH-BFL, turns on to the threshold of runway 24L in preparation for its long flight home to Amsterdam with KL 602.

Below:
Recently converted from flying passengers to a cargo configuration, this Thai Cargo Boeing 747-200 is shown here while loading. This aircraft, N522MC, is owned and operated by Atlas Air of New York on behalf of the Thai carrier.

Opposite Above:
During the year many charters are flown into Los Angeles carrying a wide variety of travellers. As the name suggests, Miami Air is based in that Floridian city and in this picture is flying on behalf of the Florida Panthers.

Opposite Below:
Based at New York's JFK Airport, Tower Air operate a fleet of Boeing 747s. Here we see N603FF about to touchdown with a flight from its home city.

MIAMI AIR
N806MA

Tower Air
Tower Air

Despite operating over two hundred Boeing 737s, Southwest Airlines presently lease four Boeing 737-300 series from American Airlines. Illustrated here is one of them, N679AA, which is parked at the new satellite area awaiting its call to duty.

Opposite Above:
Northwest's Boeing 757-251 N504US, appropriately named *City of Los Angeles*, has landed with a flight from Minneapolis and taxies to its gate at Terminal 3.

Opposite Below:
German Airline LTU Süd is based in the City of Munich and flies charters carrying holidaymakers to many parts of the world. In this instance LAX is the choice of the tourists aboard this Boeing 767-300, registered D-AMUR.

NORTHWEST
6R - 24L

LTU
LTU SÜD

226
Air Canada

QANTAS
LONGREACH
THE AUSTRALIAN AIRLINE
S
E

Opposite Above:
Air Canada's Airbus Industrie A320 C-FKOJ taxies to the gate with the daily flight from Montreal.

Opposite Below:
Having arrived early in the morning from Sydney, this Qantas Boeing 747-400 is towed to a parking space for a few hours in order to release a gate at the terminal before its departure later in the day.

Above:
American Trans Air's Boeing 757-28A N521AT is in take-off mode as it gathers speed down runway 24L. This particular aircraft is still in the colours of its former owner, Monarch Airlines of Luton, England.

Above:
Two Mexicana Boeing 727s stand at their respective gates for loading prior to departing to their Mexican destinations.

Opposite Above:
The imposing front end of a Boeing 747-400 series is well illustrated in this picture of Malaysia Airlines after its arrival on a flight from Kuala Lumpur, Tokyo Narita and non-stop across the Pacific.

Opposite Below:
Lufthansa's daily flight from Frankfurt, LH 450, is in the final stage of landing. Boeing 747-430 D-ABVA is the aircraft in charge after a long Trans-Atlantic/North American flight.

malaysia
Kuantan

Lufthansa
D-ABVA

MEGATOP
SINGAPORE AIRLINES

swissair
AA
AA
American

Opposite Above:
There are two flights per day from Singapore to Los Angeles flown by Singapore Airlines. The first flight, SQ 12, touches down on time after its non-stop sector across the Pacific from its stop in Tokyo. 9V-SPH, a Boeing 747-412, is the aircraft involved.

Opposite Below:
With a scheduled flight time to Zürich of 11/12 hours, Swissair's MD-11 HB-IWC climbs steeply on take-off from runway 25R at the beginning of its homeward journey. Behind, are the new Control Tower and Theme Building.

Above:
One of the world's busiest airports for cargo and mail, LAX is served by many international cargo airlines in a rapidly growing market. An example is Nippon Cargo Airlines of Japan. Their Boeing 747 freighter arrives in the early evening and taxies across runways 25L/R to reach its unloading area.

POLAR
POLAR AIR CARGO
N851FT

KALITTA
AMERICAN INTERNATIONAL AIRWAYS
N103CK

Opposite Above:
Polar Air Cargo, with its head office down the road in Long Beach, have twelve Boeing 747 freighters which are used on scheduled and chartered cargo flights to many parts of the world. Another flight over, this aircraft taxies to the cargo area for unloading.

Opposite Below:
With headquarters in Ypsilanti, Michigan, American International Airways is a cargo-oriented airline. With their very attractive red and gold cheatline they were the first company to use L1011s in a pure cargo layout. This aircraft, N103CK, flew for British Airways carrying passengers before its conversion to cargo configuration.

Below:
N727VA, a Boeing 727, is operated by Carnival Airlines of Fort Lauderdale, and sits at the charter terminal having unloaded its passengers.

Philippine Airlines now use MD-11s on their route across the Pacific from Manila with a stop in Honolulu. N275WA is the aircraft featured here.

This L1011-500 TriStar is part of a fleet of aircraft used exclusively by the Saudia Royal Family and members of their government. HZ-HM5 visited LAX in April 1997.

Below:
Delta Air Lines use their McDonnell Douglas MD-11s on Pacific routes out of LAX to Japan and Korea.

Opposite Above:
Hawaiian Air now operate a fleet of ex-American Airlines DC-10-10s on services between Los Angeles and Honolulu. This example, N161AA, waits after some light maintenance for its next trip to Hawaii.

Opposite Below:
EL AL operate Boeing 747-458s on their long-haul international services. The example shown here, 4X-ELC, proceeds slowly down the taxyway before departing on runway 24L on its return to Tel Aviv via New York.

HAWAIIAN

EL AL
Y 6R-24L

United Shuttle, the low-cost, no frills operation of United Airlines paint their B-737s in a different scheme to the parent company as illustrated on N358UA.

One of America's oldest airline companies Trans World, or TWA, still evoke a romantic image of days gone by. Despite some difficult times they are still flying, as this L1011 recently arrived from St Louis illustrates.

Below:
With its engines in reverse thrust for braking, Cathay Pacific Cargo touches down after its flight from Hong Kong. One of two Boeing 747-467 freighters flown by the company, VR-HUH still sporting the older-style colour scheme will proceed to the cargo area for unloading.

Opposite Above:
Another example of Western Pacific's theme advertising is well illustrated with the popular TV cartoon *The Simpsons.* Boeing 737-301 N949WP is the aircraft concerned.

Opposite Below:
One of many B-737s flown by United Airlines, this 500 series N955UA taxies to the United Terminal.

N949WP
THE Simpsons
Western Pacific
FOX

N955UA
UNITED AIRLINES

American Airlines' MD-83 N571AA is being prepared for flight AA1654, the 10.40 am departure to Chicago O'Hare, prior to passengers boarding.

British Aerospace Jetstream 31s are loading with passengers prior to departing on United Express commuter flights.

Above:
Continental's MD-80 has been pushed back from the gate and is now ready to receive instructions to taxi to its departing runway.

Left:
The tail section of a Delta MD-11 is shown against the new Control Tower.

Brazil's national carrier VARIG fly regular services from Rio de Janeiro to Los Angeles utilising their Boeing 747-341 aircraft. This picture illustrates the front-end portion of their jumbo jet.

A Malaysian Boeing 747-4H6 registered 9M-MPA has been pushed back and is waiting for instructions from Air Traffic Control to move forward and taxi to its take-off position on runway 24L. After crossing the Pacific, a stop will be made in Tokyo before the final destination of Kuala Lumpur.

'Tails' – China Airlines, Lufthansa and Korean Air B-747s are lined up side-by-side at the Tom Bradley International Terminal.

Virgin
KLM
virgin atlantic
G-VTOP

TWA
TRANS WORLD
N601TW

Opposite Above:
Virgin Atlantic, the successful British airline run by entrepreneur Richard Branson, fly a daily service to Los Angeles from London's Heathrow using the latest Boeing 747-400s.

Opposite Below:
N601TW illustrates the new colour scheme being adopted by Trans World. This Boeing 767-231 will operate a flight to St Louis, Missouri.

Above:
Los Angeles is once again visited on a daily basis by the reborn Pan Am. Airbus A300 N862PA is ready to taxi to the threshold of runway 24L in readiness for its early morning flight to New York's JFK Airport.

The new FAA Control Tower opened in March 1996. At a height of 277 feet it gives Air Traffic Controllers unprecedented views of the airport and utilises state-of-the-art equipment. Skywest's EMBRAER Brasilia twin-prop commuter aircraft are dwarfed by the tower.

This photograph taken from the old Control Tower shows the Theme Building built in 1961 and now designated as a City Cultural and Historical Monument. Rising behind, at a height of 277 feet, is the new FAA Control Tower opened in March 1996.

Above:
The Simpsons are at the gate awaiting their passengers for the return flight to Colorado Springs

Opposite Above:
A British Aerospace Jetstream 32 operated by Trans States Airlines to fly commuter services for USAir awaits its next flight to Palm Springs.

Opposite Below:
A Continental Airlines DC10-30 stands outside the company's maintenance hanger where it receives attention to its tail-mounted engine.

TRANS STATES
N871JX

Continental
C B16 →

A striking view of the front end of a VASP MD-11.

Continental's Boeing 737-3T0 N12313 is seen here on the taxyway connecting the south side of the airport to the north.

UNITED EXPRESS

NORTHWEST

Opposite Above:
A United Express Jetstream 31 arrives with another inter-Californian commuter flight.

Opposite Below:
Sporting its striking red and grey colour scheme, Northwest's DC-10-40 N145US makes its way for take-off with flight NW933, a non-stop service to Honolulu.

Above:
United Airlines Terminal is busy with two Boeing 747s and a DC-10 waiting at their respective gates while they load with passengers. This photograph was taken atop the old Control Tower, now used by the Department of Airports.

The tail section of this VASP MD-11 registered PP-SPE looks very impressive whilst being loaded for its flight to Rio de Janeiro.

Asiana flight OZ 202 has arrived from the South Korean capital, Seoul, and now waits for the tow tractor to be attached to pull it into the gate. This aircraft is a Boeing 747-48E registered HL-7416.

Opposite Above:
Air Canada's Airbus A320 C-FTJR is pushed back from the gate prior to a flight to Montreal.

Above:
Behind the tail of a FedEx A310 is Hangar No 1 built in 1929 and the first structure at the new field. Refurbished in 1990 it is registered as a National Historic Landmark and is still in use to this day.

Opposite Below:
Sun Country's colourful DC-10 sits on the ramp while it is made ready for the next flight. Based in Minneapolis, this company primarily flies holiday charters to many points within the USA and Caribbean.

AIR CANADA
C-FTJR
216
Asiana

Sun Country
6
3

Above:
United Express EMBRAER Brasilia is dwarfed by the Boeing 747s parked in the background as it proceeds to its gate.

Opposite Above:
Southern Air of Miami operate cargo flights from Los Angeles to Sydney on behalf of the Australian airline Qantas. This refurbished DC-8-73CF N874SJ will operate today's flight down under when loaded.

Opposite Below:
In February 1997 USAir renamed the airline and introduced a new corporate image. Known as US Airways its fleet of aircraft will gradually be repainted in this very attractive scheme. Boeing 757-2B7 N633AU is at the gate in the new colours.

SOUTHERN AIR TRANSPORT
U·S AIRWAYS
12

NORTHWEST

AMERICA WEST
N643AW

Below:
Sam's Town Casinos is the theme on Western Pacific's Boeing 737-3Y0 N956WP parked at the gate, loading passengers prior to flying to Colorado Springs.

Opposite Below:
America West of Phoenix, Arizona, are currently repainting their fleet in a new corporate scheme. Airbus A320 N643AW displays the new colour scheme and has just arrived from Phoenix.

Opposite Above:
Northwest Airlines have been experimenting with various changes to their standard colour scheme of red and grey. This Boeing 757-251 N534US is shown with an all-grey fuselage with the red missing.

BRITISH AIRWAYS

XA-RRY
AERO CALIFORNIA

Opposite Above:
Boeing 747-436 G-BNLC of British Airways having landed on runway 25R taxies across to the north side of the airport to its terminal after flying from London Heathrow.

Opposite Below:
The colourful livery of Aero California is well illustrated in this picture of DC-9-15 XA-RRY. In push-back mode this aircraft will shortly fly to La Paz, Mexico. Aero California is based at Baja, California.

Above:
Canadian Boeing 737-275 C-GKPW is one of many operated by Canada's second largest airline and will shortly depart on its flight to Vancouver.

Air France flight AF 064 lands at LAX with the direct service from Paris, Charles de Gaulle. This Boeing 747-228B F-GCBB is a combi-aircraft carrying around 250 passengers and 7 pallets of freight.

Air Pacific, the national carrier of Fiji, use their Boeing 747-238B DQ-FJE painted in this colourful style on services to LAX from their tiny Pacific island. After departing from the terminal, instructions are awaited from the Control Tower to proceed to runway 24L for take-off.

Frontier
The Spirit of the West
N303FL

Alaska
N979AS

Opposite Above:
Denver-based Frontier Airlines have adopted a policy of painting wild animals on the tails of their Boeing 737s. In this take-off picture it is the grizzly bear which is featured.

Opposite Below:
Regular flyers into Los Angeles, Seattle-based Alaska Airlines use a modern fleet of both MD-80s and Boeing 737s. N979AS, an MD-83, makes its way to the gate for unloading.

Above:
The 'Lone Star' symbol of the State of Texas features on this Southwest Boeing 737 and is one of several painted by the company with an overall theme.

Above:
All Nippon's daily flight NH006, a non-stop service from Tokyo's Narita airport, touches down with Boeing 747-481 JA 8296 in charge.

Opposite Above:
American Eagle's Saab 340B N349SB leaves the terminal for yet another short commuter flight.

Opposite Below:
Milwaukee-based Midwest Express MD-88 N601ME arrives with the morning flight from that city.

American Eagle
N349SB
SDL

MIDWEST EXPRESS
Y
6R - 24L

An American Airlines Boeing 767 is being prepared for its next flight as it sits at the gate. These aircraft form the mainstay of the company's long-haul flights.

Los Angeles City Fire Department maintain an impressive array of fire-fighting equipment at the airport to cover any eventuality. Crash tender No 3 is such an example and is on permanent stand-by.

Merida
MEXICANA
STOP
FOR
AIRCRAFT

LanChile
LanChile

Opposite Above:
One of Mexicana's Boeing 727s XA-MEZ and named *City of Merida* makes its way to the terminal after arrival.

Opposite Below:
With the Tom Bradley International Terminal in the background, a Lan Chile Boeing 767 waits for taxi instructions from Air Traffic Controllers before commencing its flight to Santiago.

Below:
Previously flown by American Trans Air and bearing their registration number N756AT, this Boeing 757-2Q8 is now flown by Aero Peru. After loading passengers at the satellite area the aircraft is pushed into position and engines started in readiness for today's flight to the Peruvian capital, Lima.

Singapore Airlines' 'Mega Ark' Boeing 747-412F is in the process of unloading at the very busy cargo area.

America's largest airline United have a large presence at LAX, flying many national and international flights. One of their many Boeing 747-422 series is parked at the gate in readiness for its next flight.

812
DELTA
MD-11
107
DELTA
9456
Dobbs

KLM
PH-BFL
Alaska

Opposite Above:
'Tails' at the Delta terminal with an MD-11 and a Boeing 767 filling the picture.

Opposite Below:
An Alaskan MD-80 is nicely framed by the tail of a KLM Boeing 747.

Above:
This busy scene taken from the Control Tower shows three Air New Zealand Boeing 747s parked side by side at Terminal 2. Other aircraft can be seen in the picture, all waiting for take-off.

Right and Below:
The interior of the Tom Bradley International Terminal is clean and bright and offers a wide selection of excellent food stalls and restaurants.

Following Spread:
TWA's new scheme is well illustrated on this MD-83 landing on runway 24R with a flight from St Louis, Missouri.

TRANS WORLD

TWA

FedEx Airbus A310 N408FE sits in the morning sun. Arriving in the early morning with its load of packages this aircraft will spend the day on the ramp before its next flight in the evening.

Mesa Airlines were operating this Beech 1900D when this picture was taken in April 1996.

Below:
Aeromexpress is a Mexican cargo operator using a Boeing 727-2K5F with an American registration, N909PG. Fully loaded with freight the aircraft is ready to go.

Opposite Above:
When push-back is complete the tractor will be detached from this USAir Boeing 767-2B7ER registered N653US, engines will be started and the flight will get underway.

Opposite Below:
Besides operating the smaller DC-9s, Aero California now fly the larger DC-9-32 series for additional capacity. XA-SWH is an example of the latter and is preparing to leave the Tom Bradley Terminal.

USAir
USAir

AERO CALIFORNIA
XA-SWH

Skywest Brasilia N221SW passes a Delta L1011 on its way to the terminal.

Still wearing United's former colours, Boeing 737-522 N915UA is one of many 500 series flown by the company.

Opposite Above:
The crisp red and white colours of TWA still look striking on Boeing 727-231 N54345 as it becomes No 2 for take-off.

Opposite Below:
Vanguard, a comparatively new airline based in Kansas City, fly scheduled services to LAX. With a fleet of Boeing 737s this 300 series N303AL is one of two presently leased from Aloha of Hawaii and is waiting for permission to commence its flight back home.

Below:
Having landed on runway 24R a Delta Boeing 757-232, N647DL, now taxies to the company terminal.

TWA
TRANS WORLD

VANGUARD
N303AL
303

For a few years Qantas used their two Boeing 747SPs painted as Australia Asia for use on their route to Taiwan. VH-EAA having arrived goes to the gate to unload. Photographed in 1996 this aircraft has now been repainted into Qantas colours and no longer flies to LAX.

With the modernisation of China gathering pace, many new airlines are being created using modern American-built aircraft. One example is China Eastern of Shanghai who fly their MD-11s to Los Angeles on a regular basis. B-2173 is being prepared for its flight home to China.

TriStar
AIR CANADA
C-FDSN
RAPTORS
206

Opposite Above:
TriStar Airlines of Las Vegas flew British Aerospace 146 jets on services into Los Angeles. N136TR is taxying for take-off on a flight to Las Vegas. Regrettably this company has ceased operations.

Opposite Below:
Airbus Industrie A320-211 C-FDSN of Air Canada rolls down runway 24L painted in the colours of Toronto Raptors, an NBA basketball team.

Above:
Among the many cargo companies flying to Los Angeles is the Dutch company Martinair. Their Boeing 747-228F. PH-MCN is a member of the fleet and is seen here parked in the cargo area.

The tails of a KLM and Virgin Boeing 747 stand out in the afternoon light.

Below:
United's Boeing 747-422 stands at the departure gate preparing for its long flight across the Pacific.

Following Spread:
EVA Air is the second major international airline of Taiwan and flies daily non-stop services from Taipei. B-16402, a Boeing 747-45E, is today's aircraft.

EVA AIR
空航榮長

Above:
With tow tractor attached, a Qantas Boeing 747-438 is moved away from its gate before the start of a flight to Sydney.

Opposite Above:
The old Control Tower is visible to the left of America West's Boeing 737-2M8 N141AW. This building is now used as offices by the Department of Airports.

Opposite Below:
An America West Boeing 757 after a flight from Phoenix taxies to Terminal 1 for passengers to de-plane.

America West Airlines
N141AW
When Performance Matters

America West Airlines
24L
STOP FOR AIRCRAFT

The Royal Dutch Airline KLM fly a daily non-stop service from Amsterdam. PH-BUN is a Boeing 747-200 series with a stretched upper deck.

Boeing 767-31AER PH-MCL, of the Dutch company Martinair, having arrived on a charter from Amsterdam with European holidaymakers makes its way to the terminal for unloading.

AMERICA WEST
Y
6R

B-16401
KOREAN AIR
AA

Opposite Above:
Boeing 737-3B7 N398US was one of America West's first aircraft to be painted in their new style in April 1996. This flight from Phoenix is non-stop to Los Angeles.

Opposite Below:
The tail of an EVA Air 'jumbo' frames the Korean Air Boeing 747-400 after its push-back.

Below:
Reno Air have a fleet of around thirty McDonnell Douglas MD-82/83s and operate many daily flights into LAX.

Japan Air fly several flights per day from Tokyo bringing businessmen and tourists alike.The Pacific is the busiest international route serviced out of Los Angeles. Boeing 747-446 JA 8081 is seen here making its way for take-off and a long Pacific flight.